ITALIAN PERSPECTIVES

ITALIAN PERSPECTIVES

An Inaugural Lecture

BY

EDWARD BULLOUGH

Professor of Italian in the University of Cambridge

*

CAMBRIDGE

AT THE UNIVERSITY PRESS

1934

CAMBRIDGE
UNIVERSITY PRESS

University Printing House, Cambridge CB2 8BS, United Kingdom

Published in the United States of America by Cambridge University Press, New York

Cambridge University Press is part of the University of Cambridge.

It furthers the University's mission by disseminating knowledge in the pursuit of education, learning and research at the highest international levels of excellence.

www.cambridge.org
Information on this title: www.cambridge.org/9781107634763

First published 1934
Re-issued 2014

A catalogue record for this publication is available from the British Library

ISBN 978-1-107-63476-3 Paperback

ITALIAN PERSPECTIVES

Inaugural Lectures, I am told, are at present at a heavy discount. Professors have of late been appointed in considerable numbers, and, unless they enjoy special celebrity, are not likely to attract an audience, except from among specialists in their particular science. Perhaps for that very reason they often choose as their subject abstruse topics of research, unintelligible to the average listener.

If I nevertheless venture to deliver an Inaugural Lecture, I do it as a duty, hoping that the aspect of Italian Studies which I wish to emphasise will be found neither too abstruse nor even too narrowly professional. My duty in this matter is dictated to me by my conviction that such an Inaugural Discourse should—in my own case at any rate —be both a personal confession and something like a statement of policy. I owe this both to the subject which it is my privilege to represent, and to the University which has honoured me with the task of representing it.

DANTE in a famous passage in the *Convivio*—which is the *locus classicus* always quoted on such an occasion—observes that "parlare alcuno di sè medesimo non pare licito", except on one or both of two conditions: "L' una è quando sanza ragionare di sè grande infamia o pericolo non si può cessare...; l' altra quando, per ragionare di sè, grandissima utilitade ne segue altrui per via di dottrina". Venturing to liken someone very great with someone very small, I submit that both these purposes are germane to my object.

I have the honour to be third occupant of this Chair. Of my two predecessors, Professor Thomas Okey delivered an Inaugural Discourse when in 1919 the Chair had been established through the munificence of the late Commendatore Serena. It was just after the close of the War. The whole political balance in Europe had shifted and Italy had emerged from the conflict as henceforth one of the "Great Powers". Known both as a champion of modern Italy, as well as a translator of Dante, he—unless I am much mistaken, the first Englishman to hold such an office in an English University—took as the burden of his lecture an appeal for the study of that modern Italy, the Italy of the Risorgimento, the Italy of his predilection, so evidently destined to play a decisive part in the future of the world.

Raffaello Piccoli, called only three years ago to occupy this post from that of English Literature in the University of Naples, chose as his subject "Italian Humanities". Many present here will remember his lecture. His tenure of the Chair was a continuous and painful struggle with illness which never allowed him to carry out such a scheme of teaching as he indicated in his discourse, which dwelt upon the intellectual bonds linking the Italy of the Renaissance and Humanism with the England of that time—a topic which had been one of his favourite subjects of research—and upon the value of humanistic studies of which he saw in Italy a special protagonist.

My own approach to the subject of Italian Studies differs—it cannot but differ—in many ways from that of my predecessors.

As some of my friends in the University know, I have passed through a kind of academic Odyssey. After a strictly classical school education, my studies here were devoted to French and German, under the oldest but one of the schemes of the "Medieval and Modern Languages Tripos", as it was then known. My interests, from my schooldays on, had been literary, artistic and critical, as well as linguistic. Philosophy and Psychology, in conjunction with my interests in Art and Literature, combined for many years in my intellectual hobby: Aesthetics. I scandalised some at that time by being the first, in 1906, to deliver a course of lectures on that suspect subject. I led a sort of "double life": while my colleagues in Modern Languages knew me to be coaching, supervising and lecturing for French and German, the original founder-members of the British Psychological Society allowed me to join that distinguished circle; practical psychologists like the late Henry Head, anthropologists like the late W. H. R. Rivers, honoured me with their friendship. I sat at the feet of my late Master, Hugh Anderson, listening to his teaching on the physiology of the central nervous system, and prepared sections of the spinal cord under his direction; even Fulbourn Asylum saw me as one of a class instructed by its then Director, Dr Rogers. Each set of my friends and colleagues knew nothing of the others, and were surprised, not to say shocked, to find me at home in all of them. Yet it was not a case of "multiple personality"; for there was in my mind a bond between all these branches of knowledge, and it was this bond, gathering and crystallising all my interests, that led me to the discovery of Italy.

Partly linguistic, partly literary curiosity

had led me immediately after taking my Tripos to devote myself to Russian. A little later Spanish occupied me for nearly two years. Combined with Aesthetics, the study of languages formed the basis of one of my main interests: Comparative Literature. The study of Art, especially of my favourites, Architecture, Sculpture and the Theatre, urged me to extend research beyond the confines of Europe. For a very special reason, which I urged in a paper published in the *British Journal of Psychology*, I gave myself up for two years, just before the War, to the study of Chinese in order to make some sort of direct contact with that civilisation. So Literature, Art, Language and Thought have always formed a single whole in my mind, to be separated only at the risk of lopsided incompleteness.

And Italian? I am almost ashamed to confess the origins of my Italian studies. At the age of thirteen I had read with ecstatic rapture Dumas' *Le Comte de Monte-Cristo*.

Fate willed that I should find in a box of old books, belonging to my mother, an Italian continuation of it. The decision was taken in a flash: I must learn Italian, and at once. I remember spending the next long vacation doing the exercises and learning the irregular verbs in an old grammar. But for the time being I got no further. Schoolwork, later University studies overlaid my first endeavours. But the ice had been broken, and the studies, whether French or German or Russian, Architecture and Sculpture and the other Arts, Comparative Literature, the history of criticism, one by one and all in combination, inevitably led me back to it. For every attempt to trace back the beginnings of almost any one line of search or interest beyond the mere data of textbooks invariably brought me back to what seemed to be its fountain-head: Italy. In this way Italy came to stand for me as the *fons et origo* in the history of ideas and in the development of our European culture.

I have been teaching here for nearly thirty years, alas, not Italian as I might have wished, but for twenty of them, first French and German, then almost only German, a little Russian, and Aesthetics. My chance to return to my old love only came with the War. Since then I have occupied myself intensively, though unfortunately not without constant interruptions, with the study of Italian. It is a shortcoming which honesty compels me to mention, for without this mention "grande infamia o pericolo non si può cessare": what for others has been the study of a lifetime has been mine for but fifteen years. At the same time, I would not have it otherwise, all things considered; for the time given to so many, only apparently divergent, interests has enabled me to approach Italy not by any of the ordinary roads, and free from that kind of single-mindedness which sees nothing beyond its special pursuit. It is not because I have studied Italian all my life, but because I have tried to cultivate so many interests, often seemingly irrelevant to it, that Italy stands for me as the focus of my interests.

It is this intellectual experience and journey which has impressed on me the *central problem* of Italian Studies, the topic which I would like to expand on this occasion: "ITALIAN PERSPECTIVES".

What do I mean by "Italian Perspectives"?

Giuseppe Baretti, who spent nearly half his life in this country and was the protagonist on the English side in the eighteenth-century battle in Italy between the "Anglomaniacs" and the "Gallomaniacs", launched in 1777 one of his famous pungent letters to M. de Voltaire on the subject of Shakespeare and the French translations of his works. In Chapter 5 Baretti raises the problem of translating from one modern language into another.* It is, I believe, one of the early contributions to the theory of

* G. Baretti, *Prefazione e Polemiche: Discours sur Shakespeare* (Laterza), pp. 244–246.

translation in the modern sense of that term.

Comment traduiriez-vous en italien ces quatre mots français: "le roi de France"?

—Rien de plus aisé dans le monde. Je traduirais: "il re di Francia".

—Il y a toutefois des cas où ces quatre mots italiens n'expriment point exactement les quatre mots français.

—Comment!—dit M. de Voltaire d'une voix rauque et d'un ton de courroux—ces deux phrases n'expriment pas toujours la même chose?

—La même chose, monsieur? Cela se peut, si par "la même chose" vous voulez dire "la même personne"; mais si par "la même chose" vous voulez dire "la même image", "la même idée", je vous réponds que cela n'est pas à beaucoup près dans certains cas....

And Baretti goes on to explain and to illustrate the entirely different mental picture called up by the words "le roi de France" in the mind of a Parisian *petit bourgeois*, seeing the King drive in state, surrounded by all his pomp and circumstance: "Ciel quel monarque! Qu'il est bon! Qu'il est grand! Qu'il est puissant!

On est bien glorieux d'être français: on est au moins son sujet, Dieu le bénisse!" and, in contrast, the image conjured up in the imagination of a middle-class Florentine:

> Fouillons maintenant dans le crâne de mon "sguaiato" de florentin, et voyons ce qu'il contient quand il dit "il re di Francia". Cela est bientôt fait.... "C'est un roi fort puissant, à ce qu'on dit, et qui fait bien souvent la guerre à l'empereur et aux anglais. Mais a-t-il dans son pays un palais aussi beau que le *palazzo Pitti*? A-t-il des plafonds peints par Pietro di Cortona? A-t-il une aussi belle galerie que notre *galleria Medici*? une aussi belle chapelle que la *cappella di San Lorenzo*?..." Venez donc me dire derechef que "le roi de France" signifie exactement et partout "il re di Francia"! Vous vous moquez de nous, monsieur de Voltaire, avec vos traductions mot-à-mot....

Baretti's conclusion is that it is fundamentally impossible to translate the poetry of one language into another. It is a conclusion which, for that matter, Dante had already reached 500 years earlier: "E però sappia ciascuno che nulla cosa per legame musaico armonizzata si può de la sua loquela in altra transmutare, sanza rompere tutta sua dolcezza e armonia".* But Baretti's argument rests on the fact that poetry is not made up of abstractions which have more or less exact equivalents in several languages, but on images and associations which inevitably differ from language to language, even—and particularly—in some of the commonest words.

Indeed Baretti could have pushed his argument very much further, if he had followed up the line he had suggested and enquired what the notions of "king", "roi", "re", "König" stood for in the minds of an Englishman, a Frenchman, an Italian or a German. Whereas for his eighteenth-century Parisian *bourgeois*, "le roi" was most probably Louis XVI, or might have been Louis XIV, or, if he knew his history, perhaps Henri II or François I, the "re" to his Florentine might have meant the King of Naples, or someone like "Re Enzo", or, if he was historically minded, the Longobard

* *Convivio*, I, vii.

Kings, or the "King of Italy" elected by the Italian nobles preparatory to being crowned Emperor, or possibly, but not quite unlikely, the Kings of Rome before the establishment of the Roman Republic by Brutus. In any case, while for the Parisian "le roi" was the embodiment of his country and nation, from the time of Louis XIV or Francis I on, a title of glory and of pride, "il re" to the Florentine of the time was essentially a foreign potentate, as likely as not a tyrant, possibly a barbarian, anyhow something intrinsically objectionable.

This is where Baretti's argument touches what I mean by "perspectives".

This sort of perspective in Italian things is essentially different from that occurring in other countries, in our own, in France, Germany, Spain, Russia. To say that, is, of course, both trite and obvious. The point is *how far different* and *different in what way*. For it is equally obvious that unless this difference is appreciated in our estimate of Italian things, it is hopeless to try to understand Italian history or events or persons or ideas. We should become the victims either of a pure aestheticism *in vacuo*, or of anachronistic fallacies, as, for instance, in conceiving Dante's plea for a universal monarchy in terms of the "League of Nations", or of misjudging the scale of events, as happened when the Tripoli war was regarded in this country merely in terms of one of our own innumerable little frontier wars.

Among many other acute observations made by Mr T. S. Eliot in his little essay on Dante occurs the following:

> What I have in mind is that Dante is, in a sense to be defined, the most *universal* of poets in the modern languages. That does not mean that he is "the greatest", or that he is the most comprehensive—there is greater variety and detail in Shakespeare. Dante's universality is not solely a personal matter. The Italian language, and especially the Italian language in Dante's age, gains much by being the immediate product of universal Latin. There is something much more

local about the languages in which Shakespeare and Racine had to express themselves. This is not to say, either, that English and French are inferior, as vehicles of poetry, to Italian. But the Italian vernacular of the late middle ages was still very close to Latin, as literary expression, for the reason that the men, like Dante, who used it, were trained, in philosophy and all abstract subjects, in mediaeval Latin. Now mediaeval Latin is a very fine language; fine prose and fine verse were written in it; and it had the quality of a highly developed and literary Esperanto. When you read modern philosophy, in English, French, German and Italian, you may be struck by national or racial differences of thought; modern languages *tend* to separate abstract thought; but mediaeval Latin tended to concentrate on what men of various races and lands could think together.*

This observation carries implications beyond the scope of Mr Eliot's immediate intention. The "Latinity" of Italian is well known and indeed obvious on the least acquaintance. But it involves consequences less commonly realised.

In the first place, this "Latinity" states not only a fact concerning the historical

* T. S. Eliot, *Dante* (Faber and Faber), pp. 17, 18.

descent of Italian speech, but describes a very real and practical quality of it. Historically, the direct development of Italian from Latin was the cause of the relatively late emergence of Italian as a literary medium: viz. Dante's "volgare illustre", distinct from merely local speech, even his own. Under the influence of his achievement and that of Petrarca and Boccaccio it came to occupy the position he had claimed for it; but its literary developments were again overlaid by the humanistic pretensions of the Renaissance which created a twofold "Literature", popular and learned, so that almost down to the seventeenth century "Italian" had a struggle for recognition against Latin, even then still regarded as the national "literary" medium for serious purposes.

At the same time, this "Latinity" of the vernacular guaranteed for it a *continuity* such as few other European languages possess. Though the speech was later much affected by classical Latin and infected by what Mr Eliot happily calls the "opacity or inspissation of poetic style throughout Europe after the Renaissance", it was not an infection of foreign origin, as proved to be in the case of other languages; and though Italian was tainted, in the sixteenth century, by Hispaniolisms and, in the eighteenth century, by Gallicisms, against which Italian writers like Parini directed their satirical weapons, it never underwent such profound changes as English or German or French between the thirteenth and nineteenth centuries. Dante's speech, for all the few archaisms of vocabulary and diction, is in essence not very different from modern Italian and is certainly a living and fully intelligible medium for the modern mind in a way in which Old French, Old or Middle High German or even Chaucerian English are not.

And, lastly, and most fundamentally, this linguistic continuity is also the outward symptom of a *continuity of culture* which again is very real and effective. The

"Latinity" of speech has been in part the safeguard, and in part the index, of a cultural continuity which goes back to Rome, the Rome of Imperial times, even Republican Rome.

This is neither a mere figure of speech, nor, as the foreign visitor is prone to imagine, a merely opportunist pose when the occasion would seem to demand an appeal to the country's great past. But Rome and her traditions are part of the mental make-up of the Italian, be he peasant or historian, in much the same way as the Baths of Diocletian, or the triumphal arch with the electric tram passing near it, are part of the street-picture which meets you on leaving the Central Station at Rome. The visitor is apt to receive at first something of an inward shock: it is the measure of his misunderstanding of the Italian "perspective", which not merely accepts, but uses and incorporates classical remains in the daily life of the twentieth century. The very real, practical and theoretical, consequences of this situation I shall endeavour to explain in a moment. Here I am only concerned to underline the fact that, if I may use the jargon of stagecraft, the "backcloth" of the Italian perspective is Rome, and that on this background Italian events, ideas and achievement must be seen to be understood.

Compared with this vista down the ages, the perspective of other countries is of much smaller range. Shall I be accused of exaggeration if I suggest that our perspective in this sense extends backwards only to about the sixteenth century: the reigns of Henry VIII and especially of Elizabeth? What lies beyond that stretch is "archaeology", to be understood with the help of commentaries and research, but irrelevant to our present life and problems. Many causes have conspired in this result: the shifting of political power, economic changes, the disappearance of feudalism, the discovery of America and of the sea-route to India, the developments of colonisation, the "New Learning", the Reformation: it is as the result of these, involving general social and cultural changes, that "modern" England begins. The War, I fear, and many of our educational developments since then, may shorten this perspective even more. Is it not true that for the present "Georgian" generation, "modern England" begins at the earliest in 1900?—It seems to me that for reasons of the same order, for a Frenchman the backcloth of his living culture is placed, under favourable conditions, at much the same distance: France, as he knows it, dates for him, at best, from the times of Francis I, more probably even from the French Revolution. The German perspective is bounded either by the reign of Frederick the Great, or by the Reformation. Russia, before the revolution, "began" with Peter the Great, say about 1700; even Ivan the Terrible seemed "archaeology". For the present generation, certainly for the next, the beginnings of "modern" Russia will be in 1917.

But for Italy none of the causes mentioned have been operative in breaking the view. Those great divisions which text-books use, between "ancient" and "medieval" and "modern" times, have little or no significance for Italy. The vista extends unbroken and continuous from the present to the times and persons of Constantine, of Trajan, of Augustus, of Caesar, even of the first Brutus, as part of the "living" Italy of to-day. This is the first element to grasp about Italian perspectives.

Lest I should be suspected of exaggeration, I venture to record two conversations I chanced to have.

The first occurred in the train between Rome and Florence, when I got into conversation with a well-to-do Frenchman—he turned out to be a farmer from the Gironde. He and his wife were returning from Rome; it had been their first journey abroad; they were delighted with their visit and thought this was the sort of thing needed to foster a better feeling between nations. Neither he nor his wife knew anything whatever about Italy. This fact, their obvious open-mindedness, and their satisfaction over their trip made them into ideal experimental subjects. In that outwardly so wildly romantic stretch up the Tiber valley, the little towns perched on the top of the hills, fortified, still sometimes bristling with their ancient towers and battlements, dominating the surrounding, largely rough and uncultivable, country, far from the river and railway, remnants of the fierce local fighting between petty communes and "signorotti" of the thirteenth and fourteenth centuries—they excited my Frenchman's lively disapproval. Why was the land not better cultivated? How silly to build those places on the top of the hills, far from water, with bad communications! I tried to explain. He waved my historical explanations aside: "Bah", he said, "nous avons balayé tout ça avec la Révolution". There was his backcloth.

The other conversation I had one day

with the driver of the electric tram which connects the little town where I lived with the nearest railway station, ten miles away. It was north of Venice: from this last spur of the foothill of the Alps, you can see forty miles away south of you Venice and her lagoons; south-west, on the horizon Padova, marked by the domes of Sant'Antonio, with the Scrovegni Chapel containing Giotto's frescoes, and, between you and the city, the old fortified Ghibelline town, Castelfranco, the home of the famous Madonna of Giorgione, looking, with its city walls and towers, like a battleship moored on the vast sea of the Venetian plain; west, nearly fifty miles away, the Euganean hills where Marius defeated the Gauls, and at their northern end Vicenza, the city of Palladio; to the north, eight miles away, a curious little building like the Pantheon peeps over the edge of the slope: it is the "tempio di Canova", at Possagno, Canova's birthplace, which contains a collection of casts, over two hundred, of all his works. The tram-driver and I conversed about local gossip and he told me that the little son of the local cobbler had met with great good fortune: having distinguished himself in the evening classes in painting and modelling, he had obtained a scholarship at the Academy in Venice, thanks to the Podestà and the town council. "Splendid", I said, "to find such local talent and to find it recognised." He also waved my enthusiasm aside, and sweeping the horizon with his hand, he remarked with a sort of polite boredom at having to explain these things to the uninformed foreigner: "Che vuole, signore? Siamo tutti della terra di Giotto, del Giorgione, del Palladio e del Canova".—That was the tram-driver's backcloth.—Indeed, the defeat of the Gauls by Marius, the ravages of Ezzelino da Romano who had his seat in the Duecento on a hill only five miles away near a village still called "San Zenone degli Ezzelini", the Castello Cornaro in the town where Bembo placed the scene of his symposium "Gli Asolani" at the court of the ex-Queen of Cyprus, are as much part of popular imagination and perspective, as "per Diana" is the local swear-word and confirmatory expletive, thanks to the temple of Diana and the baths dedicated to her, at the spot where now the local Cathedral stands.

This superimposition of the Cathedral upon the ancient site of classical antiquity, there as in numberless other sites all over Italy, is the symbol of Italian culture and tradition. For the "Latinity", the tradition of classical antiquity is but one strand of it; the other is the tradition of Christianity. The combination of the Roman Empire and the Christian Faith, destined together to transform the older Europe, and to build the main structure of its new civilisation, must have appeared at first sight so staggeringly improbable that we may well be pardoned for regarding it, as Dante did, as providential. The Christian tradition—this is one of the points I should like to underline—did not by any means signify either a break with or even an antagonism to Italy's classical "Latinity". On the contrary: here as elsewhere in Italian history the elements of continuity are infinitely more important than the occasional conflicts which were inevitable in the incorporation of these two forces in each other. However revolutionary Christianity was, when it impinged on the structure of the Roman state, however irreconcilable its principles were with the deification of Roman Imperial power, however uncompromising its hostility to some of the pagan practices and excesses, Christianity showed a willing acceptance of the greater and more essential elements of the ancient civilisation. In the long run it was precisely Christianity which saved these essentials: not only classical literature and art, but Roman administration and above all Roman Law, and whatever Greek philosophical and scientific genius had handed on to Roman culture.

Thus Christianity and the Church helped

to ensure the continuity, in part acting as the vitalising, progressive principle in the decaying civilisation of older Rome, in part preserving in a steadying equilibrium the elements capable of survival and directing them into the paths of a reconstituted order, after the floods of barbaric invasions and the chaos of the migration of nations. This period of salvage and rebuilding was what we commonly call the "Dark Ages"; it is the continuous transition from antiquity to the Middle Ages, preventing the kind of rupture, which occurred in North Africa, for instance—an extermination of ancient culture which barbaric dominations without the restraint and guidance of the Church might easily have inflicted on the whole of Europe.

Now, to live in a cultural world which embraces in its perspective European history from the foundation of Rome onwards, without breaks and divisions, moreover linguistically accessible over its whole range relatively speaking even to the uninstructed—about this I could tell of yet other conversations—and therefore not merely a matter of archaeological interest, means living in a world of essentially *different scale*, compared to worlds of smaller range. The consequences of this fact are clearly evident in some manifestations of this continuity.

The first consequence is a *sense of tradition* even more deeply rooted in Italy than in our country. By this sense of tradition I mean an intellectual and moral awareness of this continuity and a certain moral responsibility of the individual and of the community as the result. It is not simply a habit of passive acceptance, for it is accompanied by an open-mindedness and an absence of prejudice towards tradition that both recognise its claims and at the same time treat it with the easy familiarity of a family possession that can be used, criticised, even temporarily set aside—but is, for all that, a possession.

This attitude to tradition affords the explanation of several features, some seemingly contradictory, which are apt to strike the foreign observer.

One is the remarkable amount of historical research that has been for centuries, and is still being carried on by local effort, notably by the numberless historical societies scattered all over the country. It is a common assertion of text-books that History came into its own only late in the eighteenth century and at the beginning of the nineteenth which, it has been suggested, ought to be called specifically the "Century of History". But History has been an interest actively pursued in Italy from the thirteenth century onwards, long even before it achieved monumental expression in 1588 in the first volume of the *Annales ecclesiastici* of Cardinal Baronius, or was outlined in the plan of a universal History of the world in the mind of Pius II. The examples of Livy and Tacitus and Sallust were not lost on their descendants, and the effects of both Livy and Tacitus on the political theories of Italy in the sixteenth and seventeenth centuries are well known.

In the same way Archaeology and the research into and care of ancient monuments preceded by far such an interest elsewhere. As early as the reign of Theodoric Rome endeavoured to organise their preservation. The first attempts at a systematic survey of Roman antiquities naturally coincide with the Renaissance and are associated with names such as Flavio Biondo, Raphael and Michelangelo. It was then also, before the end of the fifteenth century, that the first Museum of Classical Archaeology in Europe was founded with the formation of the "Museo Capitolino" by Sixtus V.

Even what we now call "literary history", which can hardly be said to have been conceived elsewhere before the latter half of the eighteenth century, is represented by two volumes published in 1723 in

Naples. The author is a Mgr Gimma and the work is significantly entitled: *Idea della Storia dell' Italia letterata.* It covers the history of Italian language, poetry, philosophy, natural science, mathematics, astronomy and even medicine, from the earliest times down to his own, crystallising it all into a veritable "Kulturgeschichte" and treating literature in the most approved nineteenth-century fashion as "the expression of national culture". It preceded by a generation Tiraboschi's famous *History of Italian Literature* which it is said to have inspired. The chronological and local coincidence of Gimma's work with Vico's vast and in some respects so curiously modern, philosophical-anthropological speculations is probably more than just chance.

This cultivation of historical interests proved a great asset to Italy and incidentally to Europe as an effective protection against the virus of eighteenth-century Rationalism, opposed on principle to an historical view of human society, and bore fruit later in the Romantic Movement.

This sense of continuity of classical with medieval and modern times must be taken into account in our estimate of such phenomena, as, for instance, the Renaissance and Romanticism.

To see in the Renaissance a revolt against the Middle Ages, the beginnings of nationalism, the return to classical antiquity and to classical scholarship, in short what has rather unfortunately and vaguely been called "Humanism", is no doubt convenient, but falsifies our view, not only by excessive simplification, but by an essentially false emphasis. Because some of the more cantankerous classical scholars collided with the ecclesiastic authorities, because the Church protested against the subversive immorality of some of the humanistic devotees, because she viewed with suspicion and ultimately with open condemnation the anti-religious exploitation of some scientific discoveries, because Lorenzo Valla discovered the Donation of Constantine to have been a forgery (yet it had been described as apocryphal before him by men like Cardinal Nicholas of Cusa and Reginald Pecock, Bishop of Chichester), because the fortunate invention of the telescope and microscope opened the way to a vast extension of physical discovery beyond the confines of medieval knowledge of the material world—to label the Renaissance because of these and other facts a "revolt" against the Middle Ages—argues a lack of sense of proportion, sometimes a lack of sense of humour. What is infinitely more important than such passing conflicts, probably inevitable in the circumstances, and what is much more vital than the tit-bits of the "chronique scandaleuse" of the time which seem for so many to constitute the essence of the Renaissance, is the continuity of the "Renaissance", so called, with medieval civilisation. What distinguishes the situation in Italy is that there the continuity is so very obvious, however more striking the contrast may be in other countries. If the Renaissance did open a new era in France, in England, in Germany, and to some extent in Spain, it was because it appeared in these countries as a conception of life different from their native traditions, as a new fashion, as new habits of social intercourse, new interests, a "New Learning" and art, precisely because they were Italian fashions and conceptions and ways of life. The Renaissance was everywhere—except of course in Italy—an Italian "cultural interference", to express it somewhat crudely in anthropological jargon. Paradoxical as it may sound, it might almost be said that the famous "Italian Renaissance", which appeared in other countries, never existed in Italy herself. If it be said that this is merely begging terms, it is well to remember that the very word "Renaissance" was an invention of Michelet in the nineteenth century and no one living in Italy during the sixteenth-century "Renaissance" used it, except Vasari who, however, mentions it (and even then not explicitly) in connexion with the change wrought by Giotto in the history of painting three hundred years before.* No wonder that all attempts to assign a time limit to its beginnings in Italy have failed, and that theories range from the year 1400 back to 1000.

It is true, of course, that the situation in Italy, intellectual, philosophical, social and political, is very different in the year 1600 from what it had been in 1300. But the closer our study of the changes which took place during these three centuries, the more must we be impressed with the continuity in the transitions, the absence of violent breaks and the almost natural passing over

* Vasari, *Vite*... (1568, vol. I, p. 119): "...egli solo...per dono di Dio quella (pittura) che era per mala via, *risuscitò*"... "...Sbandì affatto quella goffa maniera greca, e *risuscitò* la moderna".... Vasari also mentions in the Proemio the "rovina e restauratione, e per meglio dire, *Rinascita*" of the arts—this latter he dates from Giotto.

from what we call the "Middle Ages" to what we call the "Renaissance"; and modern research is happily more and more coming to realise this fundamental fact.

One of the chief reasons for this insensible shifting is the very obvious fact that, given the perspective of the Italian, classical antiquity and culture did not burst upon him as the discovery of a new and hitherto almost unsuspected world, but was rather the recovery, as far as it was an extension of medieval knowledge, of his *own national past*. It is a confirmation of this fact that some of the most ardent "humanists" were also among the most ardent reformers and champions of the Italian vernacular, and that the famous, not to say notorious, "Aristotelian theory of Tragedy" was elaborated by them in the sixteenth century not as a piece of crabbed scholarship, but from a genuine desire to reform their native poetry and bring it again into contact with the deeper issues of life. It is also a curious fact that, wherever, then or later, an opposition to the "Italianism" of the Renaissance arose in other countries, it was apt to take the form, within the limits of classical scholarship, of a militant "Hellenism" to set up against the "Latinity" of Italy.

Similarly our view of the Italian *Romantic Movement* cannot find its right setting outside this same continuous perspective. Romanticism is very commonly defined as the opposite to Classicism and as a return to native poetical traditions. But it must be evident that in Italy Romanticism cannot bear this meaning, since Classicism is for the Italian precisely the native tradition. One means of avoiding the difficulty has been to deny straightway that there ever was an Italian "Romantic Movement" in the face, I am bound to say, of obvious facts of literary history and plain statements of the Italian Romantics themselves. But for this very reason the study of Romanticism in Italy is in more than one way fundamental to its study elsewhere. We may sarcastically take refuge in the witticism of Stendhal: "Le romanticisme est l'art de présenter aux peuples les œuvres littéraires qui, dans l'état actuel de leurs habitudes et de leurs croyances, sont susceptibles de leur donner le plus de plaisir possible. Le classicisme, au contraire, leur présente la littérature qui donnait le plus grand plaisir possible à leurs arrière-grands-pères".* But our satisfaction may be tempered by the knowledge that Stendhal plagiarised this remark almost literally, as he did so much of his contribution to Romanticism, from Ermes Visconti, one of the Romantic circle at Milan.†

The Italian attitude to this classical and medieval tradition is, as I said earlier, like that towards a treasured family possession, treating it with easy familiarity, free from sentimentality, even with what to an outsider may seem at times cynical

* Stendhal, *Racine et Shakespeare* (Chap. II).

† Cf. Benedetto, *Ermes Visconti*, 121.

indifference. I think that foreign visitors in Italy have often been shocked at the apparent neglect of ancient remains, the practical and sometimes degrading uses to which they have been put, the ease with which they have been set aside to make room for more urgent needs of the present.

This freedom in dealing with tradition has always been characteristic of Italy. Classical models have never exercised that spell and that sacrosanct authority in Italy which they have held elsewhere. There was the revival of the esteem for the vernacular in the full tide of humanistic enthusiasm; there were anti-classicists, who, with all respect for the classics, protested against a senseless imitation of them; in the midst of the fervent elaboration of the Aristotelian theory voices were raised against its application on the ground that what applied to Greece 500 B.C. need not necessarily apply to the Cinquecento—an argument which is always supposed by the Germans to have been invented by Herder in the eighteenth century.

Again when we encounter the famous "Quarrel of the ancients and the moderns" linked with the equally famous "Homeric question" in practically all countries of Europe in the late seventeenth century, we find the beginnings of it all in Italy in the person of that "spirito bizarro", Alessandro Tassoni, who in the last chapter, "Degl' Ingegni Antichi e Moderni", of his *Pensieri Diversi* in its edition of 1620, argues formally against an unconditional surrender to the ancients. And somewhat later, when the trouble culminated in the Romantic quarrels, the Italians hoisted their opponents with their own petard, by arguing that, if the ancients had been so great, it was due to their being allowed to be original: so the Romantics were after all merely "imitating" the ancients by claiming the same latitude.

It would be interesting to observe the working of this balanced attitude to Tradition, this peculiar blend of continuity and originality which constitutes true progress, in other provinces of culture: in Art, as it affects, for instance, the vexed problem of the "Baroque", or the influence, so widely modified in various ways, of Vitruvius, the pendant in Architecture to Aristotle's *Poetics* in the history of the Theatre; in Philosophy, especially in the disputes between Platonism and the various forms of Aristotelianism at the time of the Renaissance. The continuity remained unbroken: Prof. E. Gilson lectured in this very University on "L'Esprit de la Renaissance et St Thomas d'Aquin"; the typical "man of the Renaissance" may be found in such a person as the friend of St Thomas à Becket, John of Salisbury, who died as Bishop of Chartres in 1180; the foundations of modern scientific thought were laid by St Albert the Great; the application of the mathematical method to natural science was introduced by Roger Bacon—ideas which were to bear their fruit 300 years later in the "Accademia dei Secreti", in the "Accademia dei Lincei" and Galileo's work. On the other hand, it is interesting to observe in so typical a product of the Renaissance work as Castiglione's *Cortegiano* the same Aristotelian-Thomistic thought as inspired Dante in his *Divina Commedia*, or to find Bembo's "theory of Love" going back to the "scientia" of St Augustine and the whole mystical tradition of the Middle Ages. But space forbids.

It is, of course, true that everything must everywhere of necessity be a combination of old and new; but in the combination of old and new, this sense of continuity and tradition is peculiar to Italy, not only in the *manner* in which the tradition functions, but also by reason of the *nature of the tradition itself*.

In most, perhaps in all, other European countries, the sense of continuity of their peoples as a force in their lives and as the main lines of their perspectives takes the form of what we are wont to call their *national* tradition. I believe we mean by this expression the continuity of institutions, laws, customs and practices which have been the result of the political consolidation of the countries and peoples as distinct nations.

What is a "nation"? The concept has so far defied definition. I am not going to try to achieve the impossible: all I wish to suggest is that, here again, we are apt to create misunderstandings, for the meaning of "national tradition" may vary from people to people.

Professor Edmund Gardner devoted the burden of his Inaugural Lecture at Manchester in 1919 to the "National Idea in Italian Literature". He traced there with his customary erudition the emergence of the ideal of a national, territorial, political unity of the Italian people. Beginning with Vergil's "Italiam quaero patriam", he traced this ideal through St Gregory the Great, Dante and Petrarca, the well-known dreams cherished by Machiavelli, the passionate appeals of Fulvio Testi to the House of Savoy, Filicaia's touching laments, and Alfieri's fierce dedication of his "Bruto Secondo" to the "popolo italiano futuro", down to its achievement in the Risorgimento.

Two facts are patent enough: the one, that from the earliest times the inhabitants of the peninsula had a sense of belonging together, of forming a whole; and the other fact, that they did not form any such whole *politically*, and apparently did not desire any such national-political unity. Indeed the local loyalties and distinctions, the attachment to local customs, speech and traditions never fail to strike any foreign visitor, and this diversity is one of the great sources of the cultural wealth of the country. The very desire for territorial-political unity emerged only very late; as a really widespread *popular* desire, distinct from that of minorities or parties, it hardly appeared before this present century. The ideal existed, of course, centuries before, as the ideal of statesmen and rulers, historians and poets; attempts are scattered throughout Italian history to secure it by the dynastic or military hegemony of some one particular state, be it Milan under the Visconti or Venice in the North, or the Anjou in the South, or Cesare Borgia, or in the form of a federation of existing states—an ideal which apparently inspired the policy of Cardinal Albornoz in the fourteenth century,* or was twice again attempted later by the Papacy as a bulwark against foreign invasions. Eventually it was the example and the pressure, whether hostile or friendly, of other, politically unified, countries which led to the formation of the "United Kingdom". Complaints of the drawbacks of disunion, satirical outbursts against the practical absurdities of territorial divisions multiply especially in the late eighteenth

* Francesco Filippini, *Il Cardinal Egidio Albornoz*, 1933, p. 332.

century, and, in the face of Austrian suspicions and Austria's active measures to maintain Italy as a "merely geographical expression", the feeling of the essential oneness of all the people of the peninsula, despite political disunion, awakened with redoubled force. Yet, was there not a profound truth in Berchet's rhetorical question: "...Se noi non possediamo una comune patria politica..., chi ci vieta di crearci intanto, a conforto delle umane sciagure, una patria letteraria comune? Forse che Dante, il Petrarca, l' Ariosto per fiorire aspettarono che l' Italia fosse una"?*

For the third, no less evident fact is that right up to this time which brought the *political* "patria" into the realm of practical ends, Italy had had for centuries a "patria comune" *culturally* by reason of her unbroken Roman-Christian tradition, a culture of such unifying power that it succeeded in fusing even the remnants of Magna Grecia, the Saracenic culture in the

* G. Berchet, *Lettera semi-seria di Grisostomo.*

South, the barbaric races in the North, the politically and militarily powerful Spanish elements in Naples and Milan together with her own into a single tradition.

A danger of misunderstanding arises here from confusing or interchanging these two conceptions of unity by the use of the single term "national tradition". By no means mutually exclusive, the two kinds of unity have all through co-existed, usually in the form of a relatively small *political* "patria"—Venice, Florence, Milan, Naples —with all its intense local loyalty, pride and attachment, grafted on the common stock of the *cultural* "patria". At times, and Italian history provides many examples, the two conceptions have been in conflict: most of the foreign dominations, Imperial-Germanic, Spanish, French, Austrian, or the attempts to force a political union by a single state or on a foreign pattern, have been the occasions of such conflicts.

The misunderstanding becomes complete when Italian culture as a whole is judged by the standard of political concepts or the norm of "national" achievements of countries which measure them by their own national-*political* traditions. This occurred notably during the nineteenth century in this country or in France, for instance, which looked down with a sort of fatherly pity upon Italy as a "backward country", because she had been slow to profit by the liberal-democratic example set by England or by the centralised imperialism of France, or had been left behind in the race for industrialisation on which so many other countries had been launched. Yet it might well be contended that hardly any other country in Europe has had so rich and varied a constitutional experience as Italy in the course of her history. This experience has ranged, not only successively, but often contemporaneously, from the free Communes which revealed their strength for the first time in Europe, when the First Lombard League vanquished the Emperor Barbarossa in the battle of Legnano in

1176, through republics on the classical pattern, and the Venetian constitution which, unique in Europe, lasted unchanged in its essentials for the best part of a thousand years, up to the various forms of "Signorie", some popularly chosen like that of Frederic of Urbino, some oppressive in their tyranny like that of the Visconti, to absolute monarchies of the patriarchal type like that of Piedmont or Naples in the eighteenth century, foreign administrations like that of Spain or of Napoleon, or the quasi-theocratic régime of the later Church State. It seems no less strange to reproach with "economic backwardness" a people so hardworking and industrious, though lacking in most of the natural resources required for "heavy industries", or a land which had been the banker of Europe, which had planned, as Venice did at the end of the fifteenth century, the Suez Canal to meet the menace to her trade by the discovery of the sea-route to India, and had accumulated by its diligence and enterprise a wealth which even to-day seems phantastic. When Wallenstein sacked Mantova in 1630, his general, Aldringer, carried off for himself a spoil estimated at 8 million *scudi** from the Ducal Palace alone, and his soldiery extorted from the inhabitants of the town a further 20 millions.† Again, the Spanish administration of Naples succeeded in extracting from the country between the years 1564 and 1642 the sum of 45 million ducats, quite apart from special imposts and "donativi" which are said in the year 1646 to have reached the amount of 116 millions.‡ Where did all this astounding wealth come from? If the charges levelled against Italy have any substance—and in some measure, of course, they have—the causes of this "backwardness" must be sought not where her critics suggest they lie, but in some other combination of factors. The first step to a just apprecia-

* Approximately equal to about 7 million pounds sterling.

† Balan, *Storia d'Italia*, VII, 244.

‡ *Ibid.* VII, 336 ff.

tion is to realise that the cultural history of Italy demands a different set of standards, and that we are dealing here with a tradition lying behind and beyond political or economic developments and embodying values which in their depth and permanence may outweigh, as they did for centuries, the expediency of territorial-political union and the practical disadvantages which local diversities and even discords unquestionably imposed.

This point will be appreciated by a moment's reflexion on what *this* kind of national tradition really involved.

To call it "national" may seem misleading, certainly paradoxical; not merely because it was a common tradition of Italian culture even at a time when, politically, there was no Italian nation, but more significantly because this tradition of the Italian people was by its very constitution also *European*. This paradox is the same as the paradox of Italian Romanticism, only on the larger scale of culture. The "universality" which Eliot notes in Dante is due not only to the language he uses, nor even to the problems he sets forth, but is due—and not only in Dante—to the fact that the "national" inheritance of Italy lies at the same time embedded in the foundations of Europe as far as the Roman-Christian tradition extended.

I would venture to illustrate my meaning by three contributions made by Italy to the patrimony of the civilised world. They seem to me—and this is my point—hardly explicable on any other view but the one I am here suggesting. The three contributions are *Roman Law*, the *Renaissance* and the *Romantic Movement*, events belonging to three very different stages of Italian history.

If I mention Roman Law rather than scholastic Philosophy as Italy's contribution during the Middle Ages, my reason is that Roman Law is more specifically part of the Italian inheritance of Rome, even though the two greatest exponents of Scholasticism at its height were both

Italians, St Thomas of Aquino and St Bonaventura of Bagnoregio. Still the other nations of the West contributed hardly less, notably our own in such thinkers as Alexander of Hales, Richard of St Victor, Roger Bacon and Duns Scotus, men who conferred on our country the flattering description of the "Island of Philosophers". But Roman Law, however much the way for it may have been prepared by the developments of Canon Law (again not a specifically Italian achievement even though Gratian, it seems, was also an Italian), is a genuine Italian contribution. It was Italy which in the words of Maitland became "the focus of the world's legal history", from the eleventh century onwards, first in Rome, then in Ravenna, finally in the first European University, Bologna, with her great school of "Civil Lawyers". Representatives of all lands came together there, forming the different "nations" which composed the "universitas". From there went out men like

Francesco Accorso, son of the famous "glossator" Accursius, called to England by Edward I and professor for some time in Oxford—the man whom you will find in Dante's *Inferno*, canto xv, 110. Yet the diffusion of Roman Law owed nothing to the political hegemony of the land that gave it birth: nothing to Italian diplomacy, or industry; nothing to Italian fashion. It became a European possession, and part of European civilisation in a way in which it might never have become, if it had presented itself as a "national" contribution of Italy, in the narrow political sense of the word.

Italy's second contribution, the Renaissance, both as a development of classical scholarship and of Art, illustrates a similar situation three or four hundred years later. It would be easy to compile a list of thirty or forty names of painters, architects, sculptors, poets, humanists, philosophers and historians between the years, say, 1494, the invasion of Italy by Charles VIII, and

1527, the sack of Rome, men and women of the stamp of L. B. Alberti, Peruzzi, Michelangelo, Leonardo da Vinci, Raphael, Cellini, Castiglione, Machiavelli, Ariosto, Palestrina, Beatrice d' Este, Vittoria Colonna, etc., known all over the world. This world-wide fame is a curious and striking phenomenon, as curious and striking as this prodigious fertility in genius itself, difficult to match elsewhere and hard to explain. It is true that classical scholarship is a general European achievement; but it is at the same time true that it is part of the Italian national tradition in a very special manner. It is true that Art was then almost the last remnant of that international unity of Europe which had existed in the Middle Ages; but it is also easy to convince ourselves of the typically Italian character of the Art of the Renaissance, if we read Vasari's diatribes against the Gothic "goffezze" of the time preceding his.* Again we encounter this peculiar

* Vasari, *Vita...*, *Proemio.*

combination of a "national" and an "European" quality, qualities so far from being mutually exclusive that it is tempting to suggest that the "European" effectiveness was due precisely to the *Italian* quality of the contribution, because it represented in some subtle way an European tradition, and at the same time was free from any national-political bias.

To mention, in the third place, the Romantic Movement in this context may seem at first sight somewhat surprising. It is not usually one of the contributions set down on the debit side of Europe in its Italian account. I am not referring here to "romantic poetry" in the popular sentimental sense of the term. The Romantic Movement was as profound a revolution in culture, as the French Revolution was in the social, constitutional and economic order, and as effectively marks off the eighteenth from the nineteenth century and even from our own. For we still live under the shadow of that movement in Art, in Literature, in History and in our whole critical outlook to an extent which is seldom realised. Hence also the unusual interest of enquiring into the origins of that revolution. What many suspected earlier has been placed practically beyond doubt by the researches of the late Prof. J. G. Robertson of London in his work on *The Genesis of Romantic Theory* in Europe; namely that the ground for the appearance of Romanticism in Europe at the end of the eighteenth century was prepared by Italy. If there is one conception rather than another that can be called essential to the Romantic "position", it is the place assigned to imagination as distinct from reason in its scheme of things. The claims and the defence of imagination as the medium of poetry is the typically Italian contribution to what proved again to be an European movement, and it is not uninteresting to observe that, when in this country the claims of the imagination were upheld against rationalistic poetics, Hurd in the tenth of his *Letters on Chivalry and Romance* (1762) put his case as a defence of Ariosto and Tasso against their rationalist detractors. But long before him Gianvincenzo Gravina had furnished in his *Ragion poetica* in 1708 the formal proof that imagination ("fantasia") is the true poetical instrument and that the correct contrary to fiction is not truth, as the rationalists had assumed, but reality, and that the rationalist identification of fiction and falsehood was a logical and psychological error. Yet he was formulating what had in essence been part of Italian poetical theory since the sixteenth century and was largely an inheritance of scholastic thought.

Would it not be possible, if I ventured into contemporary life, to point to the Fascist movement as to a fourth illustration of my thesis? Unlike the others, it is too close to us and is still too much in the making to allow us to form a conclusive opinion; but Fascism seems to me to present again the same combination of national and European qualities, besides being the attempt, on a larger scale than ever before, to re-integrate the political and the cultural unities of the country. To select but one of many achievements: the Lateran Treaty of 11 February 1929 illustrates both these aspects: the healing of an internal breach, moral and cultural, of more than half a century's standing, and the settlement of the relations between Church and State by a Concordat which has become the model for nearly a dozen similar Concordats concluded since then in many parts of the world.

To quote again Eliot: "Rossetti's 'Blessed Damozel', first by my rapture and next by my revolt, held up my appreciation of Beatrice for many years".* Misconceived perspectives even when inspired by the best of intentions have stood more than anything else in the way of a right apprecia-

* T. S. Eliot, p. 48.

tion of things Italian, like this peculiar Pre-Raphaelite bias of perspective in regard to Dante, like what might be called the "Mancunian" view of the Risorgimento, or the approach of J. A. Symonds to the Renaissance. Justified no doubt from the angle of their particular points of view, the angle itself fails to take in what is essential. For any Italian achievement of any magnitude bears not only its Italian, "foreign" aspect, but has at the same time, and because it is Italian, a wider significance which attaches it to the very foundations of our European civilisation. It assumes thereby a familiar, almost homely, meaning for those whose culture belongs to that same tradition.

How can we ever hope to *teach* this sort of perspective and to convey to others this almost indefinable quality of Italian things? It is a question which impresses any teacher of experience by its gravity, for it is a problem which does not present itself in the same manner, nor with the same urgency or difficulty in any of the other branches of Modern Language teaching. The other civilisations are so much more easily accessible to the student because they have so much more in common in the shortness of their perspectives, whereas Italian—and herein lies its chief value educationally—expects him resolutely to penetrate beyond the customary range and to assimilate a point of view from which he has been estranged.

No doubt much could be done in school, and it is earnestly hoped that some practical steps may be taken to meet the demand for instruction in Italian which unquestionably exists. Especially if we who still possess a classical tradition approach it from the classical end and bring it into relation with the teaching of Classics, linguistically in particular with Latin, the pupil would be greatly helped towards a right approach to the Italian perspective.

But in its essence it is a matter which

must be left to the University. It is only at that stage that a sufficient breadth of outlook, a sufficient maturity, if not of judgment at least of interest, may be expected and developed. School-teaching can help over the first great stile: the language. Italian has a natural appeal to young people; its poetry appeals to children without difficulty; its imaginative literature was the nursery reading of our grandfathers and grandmothers; the country is a paradise for tourists—"das schöne Land, wo die Zitronen blühn"; its museums are the Mecca of artists and archaeologists. But it is a great mistake to think of Italian things as made only for children or only for enjoyment. There is a strange and arresting seriousness about them, a "grown-up" quality, of a wisdom of century-old experience, compared with which many other things seem childish and mere pastimes. As in its people sweetness, humour and an exuberant vitality are combined with hard-headed directness, so its façade of beauty and romance masks an intense earnestness and even austerity. "Quanta gloria—quanta malinconia", a woman of the people once said to someone at the height of fame and success. "Quanta gloria—quanta malinconia": it takes more than a schoolboy's mind to measure the depth of that remark of one whom we, in this country, might call an uneducated, perhaps illiterate woman.

If we then stress the old-standing friendship which has linked our countries for so many centuries, if we explain how much of our institutions and customs owe their foundations to Italy: banking terms, business jargon, nautical and naval words and things, exploration and military science, scientific research, the Royal Society, the discovery of electricity—John Cabot the Venetian and a glory of Bristol, Panizzi, the Librarian of the British Museum, Volta; if we think of parlour-games which almost all came from Italy; if I recall that "rugger" was the national Florentine sport in the seventeenth century and was ordered by the paternal government of Venice to be played by the young gentlemen in the squares of the city to keep them fit during the winter months—all these things are no doubt intimate links. Yet they are perhaps after all only the symptoms—of something much more deeply seated, much more elemental and vital. But to reach that deeper level something more is needed than the mere acquisition of facts; the acquisition of a temper of mind is needed, and of an angle of vision capable of capturing not merely the material or even the aesthetic, but the deeper significance of things Italian, their relevance to a fundamental tradition of Europe as a whole, their connexion with the Latin and Christian tradition of its civilisation.

Printed in the United States
By Bookmasters